How To Become a
Firefighter

Paul Barr

How To Become a Firefighter
by Paul Barr

ISBN 978-1-926917-11-5

Printed in the United States of America

Copyright © 2010 Psylon Press

Image on page 38 copyright © Getty Images

Neither the author nor the publisher assumes
any responsibility for the use or misuse of
information contained in this book.

Other books by Psylon Press:

100% Blonde Jokes
R. Cristi
ISBN 978-0-9866004-1-8

Choosing a Dog Breed Guide
Eric Nolah
ISBN 978-0-9866004-5-6

Best Pictures Of Paris
Christian Radulescu
ISBN 978-0-9866004-8-7

Best Gift Ideas For Women
Taylor Timms
ISBN 978-0-9866004-4-9

Top Bikini Pictures
Taylor Timms
ISBN 978-0-9866426-3-0

Cross Tattoos
Johnny Karp
ISBN 978-0-9866426-4-7

Beautiful Breasts Pictures
Taylor Timms
ISBN 978-1-926917-01-6

For more books please visit:

www.psylonpress.com

TABLE OF CONTENT

Types of Firefighters   39

Glossary   55

Conclusion   71

INTRODUCTION

Firefighting is an exciting and popular career option. As such, it is also highly competitive. In order to become a firefighter you must undergo rigorous training and meet certain requirements. The benefits to this career can be immense; including both financially and personally.

Have you always dreamed of being a firefighter? If so, there are many exciting career options and paths. In this guide, we will walk you through the various requirements for becoming a firefighter, the types of training involved and what you can expect from this career. We will also discuss the many different types of firefighting career options that are available.

Ready to begin planning your future career as a firefighter?

Let's get started!

CHAPTER 1

Getting Hired as a Firefighter

Steps to Becoming Hired

The process of being hired as a firefighter can one that is lengthy and time consuming. Making sure that you are well-prepared and understanding the many and various steps of the process can help to ease the way.

There are two ways in which you can typically submit an application to become a firefighter. You might find openings for firefighters in the classifieds section of your local newspaper and elect to apply or you might start the process by procuring an application submitting it with the hope that a position will open sometime in the future. In either case, obtaining an application is the first major step. You can typically obtain an application as well as relevant information regarding the exam as well as the local hiring process from your local fire department or from your city's department of personnel.

The next big step in the process of becoming hired as a firefighter is to take a written examination. This test is usually fairly complex and typically lasts around two hours. The test is commonly comprised of around 100 multiple choice questions. The questions are designed to test your understanding regarding spatial orientation as well as your memory and powers of observation, your knowledge of tools, ability to read and understand written directions, etc. If you score high enough on the written exam, the next step in the process will be an oral interview. A committee that consists of the fire chief, a representative from the city's personnel or HR department and possibly local business people handle the interview.

You will also need to undergo a physical fitness test that includes conditioning exercises and engine work simulation tests. These tests include carrying a hose upstairs, dragging a hose, ladder work and ladder ascent and descent. Each of these tests are designed to be completed without pause and must be completed within a specified amount of time.

In addition, you will need to undergo a background investigation as well as a psychological evaluation. The psychological evaluation is conducted due to the danger and hard work involved in firefighting. Firefighters commonly work at tremendous heights and often in confinement as well as inclement weather. Fire departments want to ensure that candidates for firefighters are mentally capable of handling the stress involved as well as various types of situation they may encounter.

A medical exam is usually the next to last step in the process of being hired as a firefighter. This is done to rule out any pre-existing medical conditions and serves as a baseline in order to detect any service related problems that may be detected during annual or periodic medical examinations.

Finally, the last step in the hiring process is an interview with the fire chief.

The Application

When contacting the appropriate agency to begin the application process for becoming a firefighter, it is important to make sure you obtain any necessary instructions for completing the application, including the correct procedure for filling it out. You should also make sure you find out how the exam notice will be made public, when the exam will be available and where information regarding the exam will be published.

Keep in mind it is imperative that you ensure the application is submitted on time. In most cities, you will be required to file for the exam by submitting your application by a specific date. If you plan to mail in the application, ensure that it is postmarked prior to midnight on the closing date that is indicated in the job announcement. Once you file for the exam, you will typically be notified by mail as to the location where you should appear for the exam. In some cities "walk-in" exams are offered. In this case you will not be required to file for the application in advance. The most important thing is to know when the exam will be given and if there is an applicable filing cut-off date. If so, you will need to make sure that you file prior to that date.

Where to Find Jobs

The first place that you should look for firefighting jobs is in your local newspaper. The Sunday newspaper is usually the best time to look as this is when most fire departments tend to post any openings they may have. If you do not live in a major city, you might also check the classifieds for openings in nearby larger cities. You might also check the jobs section at www.firehouse.com. Keep in mind that openings may be listed in cities far from your current location and you will need to determine whether you are willing to relocate. If you are willing to relocate your chances of finding a job will dramatically increase.

If you do not have any experience in firefighting it is a good idea to consider taking fire courses that may be available at your local community college or possibly through fire associations. This can help to give you some inside knowledge and training. Furthermore, many such courses are often taught by people who actually work within a fire department and who may be able to tell you of possible openings. In addition, taking such classes will give you the chance to network with other people who may also be looking for firefighter jobs.

Yet another good place to look for possible job openings is within the classified section of fire magazines and trade publications, such as Firehouse Magazine. Entry-level firefighter positions are sometimes listed in such publications. These magazines provide a great opportunity to learn more about firefighting as well as possible advertised positions.

Firefighter Job Requirements

Along with the standard firefighter job requirements there are often certifications that you must have in order to be considered for a firefighting job. Since September 11, 2001 the competition for firefighting jobs has become extremely fierce and intense. Consequently it is no longer simply enough to have the physical abilities and desire necessary to become a firefighter. You must also make sure you stand out from the competition and one way to do that is by obtaining certifications. Certifications which you should consider obtaining in order to become a firefighter include:

- EMT certificate
- Paramedic license
- Clean drivers license record
- EMT experience in a hospital or ambulance-full-time or part-time.
- CPR for the Professional Rescuer (American

Red Cross) or CPR Healthcare Provider
- (American Heart Association)
- Firefighter 1 Academy Certificate and/or Firefighter 1 State Certification
- Ambulance Drivers license

In addition you should also have excellent physical fitness. Weight lifting alone is not enough. You must also be fit in terms of aerobic activities and cardiovascular abilities.

Volunteer experience is also important. Many small municipalities and counties are often looking for volunteer firefighters. You might consider contacting your local fire department to find out if they have a need for volunteer firefighters. It is also a good idea to contact the local fire department to find out whether they have a need for volunteers for non firefighting capacities such as hazmat training, administration, fire prevention, etc.

In addition, specialized training certificates can also prove to be helpful. These certificates include:

- Public education
- Fire prevention
- Fire investigation
- Auto extraction
- Rescue systems
- Swift water rescue
- Hazardous Materials First Responder

Keep in mind that many cities also give preference to candidates who speak a second language, particularly Spanish. Bilingual ability in any other language; however, can help you to stand out from other candidates.

It is also a good idea to go ahead and take steps to become involved with different organizations related to firefighting. Such associations include:

- State Firefighters Association
- International Association of Arson Investigators
- National Fire Protection Association
- National Association of EMTs
- Fire Service - EMS Publications

Additional Ways to Prepare to Become a Firefighter

The best way to prepare to become a firefighter and take the firefighter exam is to spend some time studying sample questions for the exam. There are many books on the market that offer sample study questions, including Firefighter Written Tests by Robert Andriuolo and Barron's Firefighter Exams by James J. Murtagh.

Firefighter Requirements

The requirements for becoming a firefighter can vary from one city to another. Below are some examples of firefighter requirements from some of the larger cities in the U.S. Keep in mind that these requirements certainly do not apply to all cities, but they will give you a good idea as to what may be required by some cities and fire departments.

Portland, Oregon

Minimum qualifications:

- Must be 18 years of age or older.
- Must be certified as a basic structural fire fighter by the Texas Commission on Fire
- Protection.
- Must be certified as an Emergency Medical Technician by the Texas Department of
- Health.
- Must possess a high school diploma or G.E.D.
- Must possess a valid Texas driver's license and pass the Class B fire fighter's exemption within the first 12 months of hire.
- Must be in good physical condition, weight in proportion to height.
- Must score a minimum of 70% on the written examination.
- Must pass the Physical Agility Examination.
- Must successfully pass an investigation

of personal history and background to determine
- suitability for the position of fire fighter with the Portland Fire Department.
- Must pass a drug screening examination.

New York City

Minimum Requirements:

- Be between the ages of 18 and 29
- Pass both the written and physical exams;
- Pass a medical exam and background investigation;
- Be at least 21 years of age;
- Be a U.S. citizen;
- Have at least 15 college semester credits earned or full time military service with an honorable discharge; or 6 months of full time, satisfactory paid work experience;
- Hold a motor vehicle driver's license valid in New York State;
- Be a resident of one of the five boroughs of New York City, or live in Nassau, Orange,
- Putnam, Rockland, Suffolk or Westchester County;
- Be a Certified First Responder with Defibrillation (CFR-D).

Keep in mind that if you would like to become a firefighter, there are also many other people with the same goals. There are typically numerous candidates for each job opening. It is not unusual for there to be perhaps at least 50 candidates who are all vying for just a handful positions. Consequently, competition for each open position can be quite fierce. In order to stand out from the competition and increase your chances of becoming a firefighter it is important to begin preparing early and earn as many certifications as possible.

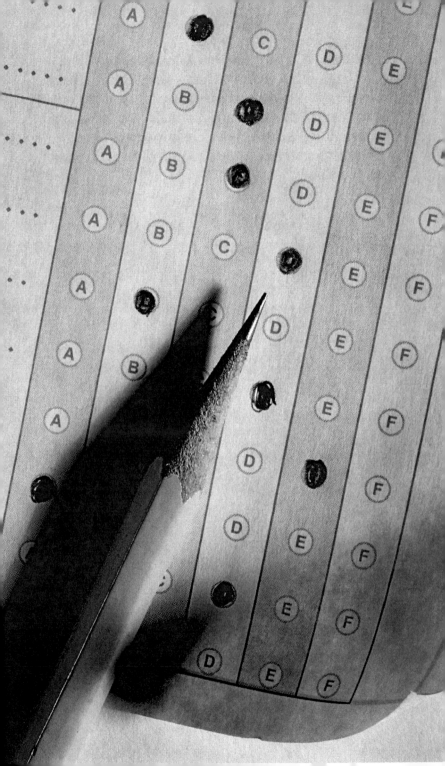

CHAPTER 2

The Firefighter Exam

What you Need to Know

You can expect the firefighter exam to take an average of 3 ½ hours to complete. There are typically at least seven different types of questions contain on the exam. The most common types of questions include:

- Visualizing, recalling and spatial orientation questions
- Verbal/listening and reading comprehension questions
- Questions on understanding and applying basic science and math
- Questions related to equipment and tools
- Questions related to dealing with people
- Questions testing judgment and reasoning

Most Common Firefighter Exams

FireTEAM

This particular exam was developed mainly as a way to prescreen entry-level candidates and also to save significant staff time that has traditionally been spent on oral interviews.

The purpose of this exam is to measure skills and abilities in four different categories, including:

- Public relations
- Teamwork
- Reading ability
- Mechanical aptitude

FireTEAM Video-Based Human Relations Test

Another FireTeam test is a video-based human relations test. This particular test is multiplechoice and is also video-based. The purpose of this test is to gauge human relations skills.

There are many areas which are covered by this test, including the following:

- Positive vs. negative influence on station internal relations
- Teamwork
- Professional responses in difficult situations
- Situational judgment
- Positive relations with supervisors and management
- Professional behavior and bearing

FireTEAM Reading Test

This test completes the elements of the FireTEAM testing battery. It is specifically designed for firefighting due to the ongoing study of technical and difficult materials. This test addresses the reading competency that is necessary for performing this job.

ErgoMechanical Animated Aptitude Test

This test is designed to address the following:

- Analytical problem solving
- Adapting and improvising
- Working with complex systems and sequences
- Understanding the physical world
- Anticipating predictable occurrences

Cooperative Personnel Services (CPS)

During the early 1990s this test was extensively used; however, since that time it has primarily been replaced in many locations by the FireTeam tests. The most common CPS written tests that might be encountered today include:

- #2129: Entry Firefighter
- #2150: Entry Firefighter
- #2158-A: Entry Firefighter (EMT / Paramedic requirements only)
- #2179: Entry Firefighter
- #2199: Entry Firefighter

Fire departments may also choose to use supplemental tests for assessing specific skills, such as the following:

- EMT
- Paramedic
- Firefighter Essentials
- Ground Ladder Practices

WH Management Solutions - Selection Solutions Entry - Level Firefighter Written Test

This is an entry-level written exam for firefighter candidates which is commonly used by many fire departments around the country. This test utilizes research on conditional reasoning and multiple intelligence along with broader job related abilities. Most entry-level written tests only measure knowledge skills; however, this test also assesses numerous other dimensions as well, such as emotional skills, practical skills, self-awareness and interpersonal skills.

Firefighter Exam Scores

Once you have taken the firefighter exam, your scores will be published or posted. Make sure you find out the process for publishing scores in your local area. If you do not achieve a perfect score the first time you take the exam and/or if you feel that you do not agree with the official answers, you may be able to file a protest. The exam instructions or the examining agency office should be able to provide you with the procedure for filing a protest.

If you do plan to file a protest, be aware that there may be a limited time for doing so. Your protest should include an explanation as to why you feel your answer selections were better than the official answer. It is also a good idea to list any reference materials that might support your claim. In the event you want to protest more than one question on the examination, you will most likely need to submit each individual protest separately. Make sure that you have signed your name as well as provided your address.

In most instances, the examining agency will review your protest and then a final determination will be made prior to publishing an official answer key. Keep in mind there could be several months between the time you take the exam and the time when the final answer key as well a s the official list are actually published. When the final list of candidates has been published, you will typically be notified by mail. At this point, the next step in the process will be the announcement of appointments for emotional and physical tests. Once again, there could be several months before this actually takes place. While you are waiting for announcements, it is crucial that you ensure you remain on top of the process. If you should happen to move, make sure you notify the examining agency and provide them with your new address.

The Oral Interview

The next step in the process of becoming a firefighter will be the oral interview. There are three basic parts to these interviews and each part is extremely important.

The interview will commonly be conducted by a board that will include the fire captain as well as personnel from the department staff, people from the local business community, community organizations and/or the local government who are all familiar with the fire department and who have experience in handling interviews.

Firefighter candidates who are serious about being hired may spend numerous hours studying for the exam. It is important to keep in mind that you should spend just as much time preparing for the interview. Making a misstep in the interview could mean the difference between being hired and being passed over.

In preparing for the interview, you should make sure you are aware of the date, time and place the interview will occur. Make sure you plan ahead and are able to arrive to the interview at least 15 minutes in advance. This will ensure that you have plenty of leeway in case of a problem or emergency. You do not want to be late to the interview simply because you had difficulty in locating a parking place. You also do not want to lose out on a position because you arrived late while another equally qualified candidate did not.

As with any interview, it is extremely important that you make a good first impression. The way in which you conduct yourself during the interview forms a large part of the impression you make. You should strive to be self-confident, alert and courteous. Make an effort to smile at least on occasion. Look each of the interviewers in the eye while listening to the questions as well as while responding. Sit up straight, but give the appearance of being relaxed. You should also ensure you are prepared to answer any question that may be asked of you.

Throughout the interview, the board will be attempting to evaluate the qualifications they feel are necessary for the job but which were not measured in the written exam. This is the purpose of the interview.

Such qualifications may include:

- Goals
- Interests
- Attitudes
- Ability to communicate orally
- Personal qualities

With that said; however, this certainly does not mean that topics which were covered in the written exam will not be questioned further during the interview.

The Physical Test

It should be kept in mind that even though firefighting remains the same across the country, it has been determined through the courts that each municipality and city is responsible for analyzing their own needs and developing a physical test that is designed to meet those needs for firefighter candidates.

The physical test is meant to measure the ability of a candidate to perform common firefighting tasks such as the ability to wear typical firefighter clothing, carry equipment weighing up to 75 pounds, etc. In order to achieve a good score on the physical test, it is imperative that you be in good physical condition and familiar with the areas in which you will be tested.

You should first determine whether there will be a training program available for the test and whether you will be able to practice with the equipment that will actually be used during the test. If you discover that is the case, it is important to make an effort to spend time at the training site. Many cities are now using the Candidates Physical Abilities Test or CPAT. This commonly involves viewing a film on the way the test is structured and what will need to be performed during the test events. If the city where you hope to be hired uses the CPAT it is a good idea to try to view the film so that you can be as prepared as possible.

Prior to taking the test make an effort to find out from the testing agency, human resources department or the fire department if there are any restrictions that will be imposed for the events of the test and if so what they are.

There are also several questions that you may wish to obtain about those prospective restrictions, such as:

- How will the test be graded?
- Will it be pass/fail test or will there be a grade?
- Will there be a set time limit for completion?
- If the test is a speed test, what time do you need to achieve to get the highest score?
- How much time can you take to get a passing score?
- What kinds of personal protective equipment will you be required to wear?
- Will this gear be excluded from use during the test?
- How can you know the beginning and the end of each event?
- What constitutes a successful completion of each test event?
- Will you the allowed a rest period between events?
- If so, how long will the rest be?

Keep in mind that in some cases the test may be comprised of a total time for completion of all events or could have a specific time for each individual event.

Many candidates make the mistake of thinking they can become prepared by simply performing exercises such as push-ups, weight lifting, etc.; however, this is rarely enough to become properly prepared. In order to be properly prepared for the physical exam you need to engage in an exercise and training program that will prepare your body for the same types of tasks that are involved in firefighting, including lifting and carrying heavy weights, running, jumping, bending, twisting, etc.

The exam itself does actually vary from one city to another, but there are some events that you can be certain you will be tested upon. They include:

- Hose/Tools Carry-This event is meant to test your ability to lift a fire hose that weighs approximately 50 pounds from an elevated position or from the floor and carry it for a distance ranging from 75 to 250 feet. You may also be required to carry the hose while climbing stairs.

- Hose Drag/Hose Line Advancement-This event is used to evaluate your ability to move a hose a distance of between 50 and 200 feet.
- Hose Advancement-This test measures your ability to work as well as drag a hose within a

confined space for at least 50 feet.

- Hose Coupling-This test will require you to attach a female hose coupling to a male coupling on a fire hydrant while you are in a standing position. It is not uncommon to be required to perform this test multiple times while also wearing a 25 pound pack at the same time.

- Hose Hoist-This test measures your ability to pull hose up the outside of the building to an upstairs floor. It is commonly performed from a standing position. In some areas you may be required to wear an air tank while performing this test.

- Stair Climb/High Rise Event-This test evaluates your ability to climb stairs while you are carrying such firefighting equipment as a nozzle, hose, hand tools, etc. You will be required to climb between three and six flights of stairs to a stop point that is designated in advance while carrying equipment that may weigh up to 25 pounds. You may be required to perform this test several times and may also be required to wear an air pack while performing this test.

- Ladder Climb-The purpose of this test is to measure your ability to ascend a ladder. You may also be required to carry tools or wear an air pack while performing this test. In addition, you may be required to dismount the ladder at an upper height, walk around the ladder and even remount and then climb back down the ladder.

- Ladder Raise-The purpose of this test is to measure your ability to lift a ladder from a horizontal position up to a vertical position. This is done by lifting the end of a ladder up to 24 feet in length and then lifting it from the horizontal position to the vertical position.

- Ladder Extension/Hoist-This test is meant to measure your ability to apply pulling force in order to raise a fly section on an extension ladder. This is performed while standing.

- Ladder Carry/Equipment Carry-During this test you will be required to begin from a standing position and lift a ladder up to 20 feet in length and then carry it to a previously designated endpoint for a specific distance. This test is meant to simulate the act of lifting a portable ladder and the transporting it to where it is needed. You will then be required to place the ladder on the ground or on a rack and then lift equipment from a cabinet, shelf or the floor and carry it for about 150 feet before returning to the beginning position and returning the equipment.

- Victim Removal/Drag-Carry-The purpose of this test is to measure your ability to pull a dummy that weighs between 110 and 180 pounds from a distance of between 50 and 100 feet. The event is meant to simulate dragging an unconscious individual from a fire.

- Search and Rescue/Obstacle Course/Confined Space or Maze-The purpose of this test is to measure your ability to navigate a confined space for a distance of up to 100 feet that may change direction and height in different locations. There may also be obstructions. This test is meant to simulate searching a fire area for a person that may be trapped.

- Ceiling Push/Tool Use-In this test you will be required to use a firefighter's hook and exert a force of up to 100 pounds upon a metal plate in the ceiling. This is meant to simulate the act of pushing a hook through a ceiling in order to prepare it for pulling it down or to locate fire burning in spaces behind the ceiling.

- Ceiling Pull/Tool Use-In this test you will use a firefighter's hook and exert a pulling force of up to 100 pounds. The goal is to be able to move a part of the ceiling downward.

- Forcible Entry/Tool Use-In this test you will measure your ability to deliver a sufficient amount of force to breach a wall or open a locked door. You will be provided with a mall, sledgehammer or axe that weighs approximately 10 pounds and then be required to hit a target horizontally using a side to side motion.

- Chop Roof or Floor Tool Use-Ventilation-This test is meant to measure your ability to apply up to 50 strokes downward using a weighted tool. It is meant to simulate the act of cutting a hole in a floor or roof.

Firefighting Equipment

Once you have actually been hired as a firefighter, the department will provide the majority of the equipment you will need to perform your job. Later you may find there is some equipment or tools that you would like to purchase to supplement your departmental supplies.

Equipment that will be supplied to you will typically include:

- Boots-these may include bunker boots, fire boots and/or turnout boots.

- Fire helmet-there are actually many different types of fire helmets that may be issued to a firefighter based on their assigned task and fire department. These include Technical rescue and USAR helmet, the traditional fire helmet with NFPA Approved Easy Flip Face Shield, the traditional fire helmet, etc.

- Fire gloves-there are also many different types of firefighting gloves including structural fire gloves, extraction gloves, technical rescue gloves, etc.

- Lights-the most common types of lights used are LED lights, many of which can create a beam for up to one mile. There are also right-angle lights, box lights, headlamps, fire and tactical hands-free lights.

- Clothing-a firefighter is also usually issued a variety of firefighting apparel, most of which will be constructed of Nomex and Kevlar. This may include protective jumpsuits, pants, suspenders, protective coats or turnout coats, rain gear, safety vests and chaps.

- Misc. equipment -other firefighting equipment typically includes firefighter bags, fire goggles, radio harnesses, hoods, air tanks, respirators, etc.

CHAPTER 3

Types of Firefighters

There are many different types of firefighters. While many people assume that firefighters commonly work out of a firehouse, that is not always the case.

Airport Firefighters

In order to cope with emergency situations, airports commonly have their own firefighting personnel. Airport firefighters are trained to extinguish structural and building fires as well as fires on board aircraft. They may also assist with rescuing people aircraft as necessary and work with situations that involve chemical hazards.

Due to the fact that there are hazardous materials, including jet fuel, which are stored at airports, firefighters working at airports may need to also cope with spills and leaks. Consequently, they must have knowledge relating to environmental hazards that may be associated with such situations and the best way to handle them.

Part of the job of any firefighter is fire prevention. This includes inspecting equipment and the airport grounds on a regular basis to identify situations that may be potentially dangerous. Airport firefighters must also inspect any facilities where chemicals may be stored. In the event a safety hazard is discovered, the firefighter must take all necessary precautions to handle the situation and reduce the chance of harm.

This type of firefighting job commonly involves working different shifts. If you are considering becoming an airport firefighter, you will need to be prepared to work nights as well as holidays and weekends as required. If there is an emergency, you may need to be on call 24 hours per day.

The first step to becoming an airport firefighter is to qualify as a regular firefighter. This means you must pass an entrance exam as well as complete required training programs. In addition, an airport firefighter must have several years of experience before they will be able to enter this type of work environment, which is considered to be specialized.

In addition, if you are considering becoming an airport firefighter, you must also obtain training in airport firefighting. In some areas, you may be able to taking courses through a local college or university. The average salary for an airport firefighter is about $37,000 per year.

Military Firefighter

The military must also have their own firefighters. Firefighters in the military perform many of the same job functions as civilian firefighters, including being call out to handle vehicle emergencies, fight natural fires, put out fires in buildings and aircraft, etc. They are also responsible for conducting inspection of fire vehicles and equipment on a regular basis.

In some cases, fire prevention demonstrations may also be part of the job duties of a military firefighter.

Firefighters in the military may also be deployed to handle spills or leaks of hazardous materials. Senior firefighters are responsible for supervising the work of personnel who are in the lower ranks and may also conduct fire investigations. This type of work can be demanding, both mentally and physically.

The training base for military firefighters is located in San Angelo, Texas at Goodfellow Air Force Base. New recruits are required to undergo 9 weeks of basic training along with an additional 13 weeks of specialized firefighting training that includes field work and classroom instruction. Training includes:

- How to operate different types of firefighting equipment
- Different types of fires
- First aid
- Firefighting procedures
- Rescue

Becoming trained as a military firefighter is an excellent way to become prepared for a career as a civilian firefighter in the future.

Women Firefighters

At one time only men were firefighters, but today that is no longer the case. More and more women are now becoming involved in this career field. Presently, there are more than 6,000 women working in fire departments around the country. Women can hold a variety of different ranks in fire departments including engineer and sergeant as well as higher ranks such as department chief.

Women who are interested in becoming a firefighter must also be in excellent physical condition and must be able to handle the physical demands of the job. Although firefighting can be a challenging career, it can also be very rewarding.

Volunteer Firefighters

Volunteer firefighters perform the same types of job duties as salaried firefighters. Around the country, there are actually more volunteer firefighters than paid firefighters. Most of the fire departments around the nation are volunteer departments.

As a volunteer firefighter you will still need to spend time training and must be prepared to respond to a variety of different emergency situations, including:

- Emergency medical incidents
- Fires
- Natural disasters
- Acts of terrorism
- Water rescues
- Hazardous material spills

Persons interested in firefighting as a career may find that becoming a volunteer is a good way to begin. The number of volunteer firefighters around the country is on the decline while the average age of individuals involved in volunteer firefighting is on the rise. This is leading to a situation where there will be more opportunities available for people who are interested in becoming a volunteer firefighter.

Young people who are interested in becoming a volunteer firefighter will find excellent resources available through the National Junior Firefighter Program.

Seasonal Firefighting

Persons who are interested in a challenging career that allows them to spend time outdoors may be interested in seasonal firefighting. Seasonal firefighters are responsible for physically carrying heavy packs with supplies and may need to hike over rough terrain for some distance. They must also be knowledgeable regarding outdoor survival skills.

Based on the situation, if you are a season firefighter you may be required to spend several days or possibly even weeks camping outdoors. The areas where you will be working may be remote. The hours are also usually long and you may be required to work up to 20 hours per day. The season typically runs from May to September.

Fireline Handcrews

A handcrew is typically comprised of between 18 and 20 firefighters who primary responsibility is putting a fireline in place. A fireline is a part of land which has been cleared of anything flammable to prevent the advancing fire from growing by feeding off of a fuel source. The handcrew must dig straight down to the soil in order to eliminate any possible fuel for the fire. This type of work can be quite demanding physically and most handcrews put in long hours. The work day for a handcrew firefighter commonly begins at dawn, when they leave camp and travel to the fire location. It is imperative for the entire crew to continually be aware of the location of the fire and the direction in which it is moving. For this reasons, there is commonly a lookout on each crew.

After the handcrew is in place, a variety of hand tools are used including shovels, chainsaws, etc. Each member of the crew is responsible for carrying a backpack that may weigh up to 25 pounds or possibly more. They may be required to hike for several miles before they reach the site where the fireline is to be constructed.

Individuals interested in this type of work must usually have some prior firefighting experience and must be able to pass a physical exam as well as a work capacity test that involves hiking three miles in 45 minutes or less, while wearing a 45 pound backpack.

Helitack Crew

The helitack crew arrives at the site of wildfires and performs much of the work related to the first line of dense against wildfires. This type of crew is commonly deployed anytime there is a need for a quick response or when the fire may be located in an area where it would be difficult to achieve access using traditional ground based transportation.

The helitack crew is first transported by air and then dropped near the site of the fire. Hand tools are used to establish a firebreak in order to stop the flames from progressing. The helicopter is also used for transporting water to the site of the fire. In the event the fire continues moving forward, the helitack crew will then support other firefighters in attempting to extinguish the fire.

Openings for helitack firefighters are usually published through the federal government. Candidates must typically have a minimum of one year of firefighting experience or a Bachelor's Degree in Forestry, Agriculture or Range Management.

Wildland Fire Hotshot Crew Firefighters

Anytime there is a large wildland fire, a hotshot crew may be sent in to help fight the fire. This is a crew made up of specialized firefighters who are organized into crews of up to 25 members. Special responsibilities of these crews may include:

- EMT training
- Cutting through brush
- Moving brush out of the way
- Maintaining water pumps, vehicles and other equipment

Hotshot crews may also assist in performing search and rescue operations. These crews commonly work in extremely rough conditions and may need to be on a field assignment for several weeks. They may work an average of 16 hours per day. It is not uncommon for a shift to last between 48 and 64 hours. Being in excellent physical condition is a must for this job. Members of a hotshot crew must be able to lift heavy weights, hike for long distances, etc.

This type of work tends to be seasonal, between May and October.

Smoke Jumpers

Smoke jumpers are specialized personnel who are trained to be deployed into remote locations. The goal is for a smoke jumping team to arrive on scene just after a wildfire has begun in an attempt to contain it before it can spread further. The smoke jumping team is transported by airplane to the location and then uses parachutes to jump to the ground. This type of work is extremely dangerous. In the event of an injury it can be a challenge to get medical help.

Once the crew is on the ground they use the same types of equipment as other firefighters including shovels, chain saws and pulaskis (a tool that has an ax on one side and a flat blade on the other side.) Crews may also be responsible for bringing in portable pumps.

Smoke jumpers wear heavy boots and padded suits. They must be comfortable with working outside and exiting airplanes with the use of a parachute. A minimum of one year of prior wildland firefighting experience is usually required. Applications can be made through the Bureau of Land Management or the U.S. Forest Service.

EMT

EMTs are also often hired by fire departments. This is because many of the calls to a fire department may involve medical situations and emergencies. The fire department is often first on the scene even before the police and the ambulance; therefore it can be helpful to know life saving techniques. All firefighters are typically required to be certified in CPR and to use defibrillation; however, it can certainly be helpful facing a situation that may require advanced medical training.

EMTs typically must take a 12 week course and have around 144 hours of training. You may also be required to take two exams; one of which is written and one of which is practical or hands-on. EMTs must keep up with training and refresher courses every two years as well as log a certain amount of hands-on training for each of those two years.

Paramedics

A paramedic is trained to respond to a variety of different emergencies including assisting in putting out fires, rescuing persons who may be trapped in burning buildings or vehicles and more. They may also assess and treat injured individuals. The requirements to become a paramedic vary from state to state. Training can last from just a few months up to four years. State exams are also commonly required. In many areas, paramedics must also keep their skills current by taking refresher courses. Tasks that may be performed in the field by a paramedic caring for an injured person include:

- Airway management, including intubation
- Administration of oxygen by mask
- Administration of intravenous fluids
- Use a defibrillator
- Monitoring an ECG reading
- Administration of medications for the control of pain, cardiac resuscitation drugs, sedatives, etc.
- Applying dressings to control bleeding
- Immobilizing patients who may have spinal or neck injuries
- Assessing and applying splints to fractures
- Assessing obstetrical complications
- Providing assistance to women in labor
- Assessing and treating burns

Career Outlook for Firefighters

Although there is significant training involved in becoming a firefighter, it can pay off. A full-time firefighter will work an average of 56 hours per week; although those work hours are usually divided into 24-hour shifts. In some departments, a firefighter may work 8 or 12 hour shifts.

While a firefighter is on duty, he/she may live and eat together at the firehouse. Instead of working their 8 hour shift and then going home, they are continually together while working. The firehouse itself commonly features an area for an office as well as a kitchen and dining area. Firefighters will commonly sleep in a dorm style type room. Shower and bathroom facilities are also available. There may also be a TV room or lounge.

All members of the crew are responsible for participating in the household chores, including cleaning and cooking. Due to the fact that crew members actually live together much of the time they must remain flexible and be tolerant of one another. They must also trust and rely on one another.

The salary for a firefighter can range from $50,000 to $65,000 per year. There is also a benefit plan available in most areas. A veteran firefighter can usually retire after 25 years of service. Due to the fact that many firefighters retire early in life, they may still be able to begin a new career after retiring as a firefighter while still enjoying a pension or retirement from the department.

Competition for firefighting jobs can be extremely fierce. Once you are hired, the job security tends to be quite good because most firefighters are never laid off due to the fact that firefighting is considered to be an essential service.

Promotion usually occurs from within; which means there is opportunity for a firefighter to move through the ranks to upper positions. The employment outlook for this industry is expected to grow at a rate that is faster than usual through the next several years, especially as veteran firefighters reach retirement age.

GLOSSARY

AIRTANKER: Fixed-wing aircraft certified by FAA as capable of transport and delivery of fire retardant solutions.

ANCHOR POINT: An advantageous location, typically a barrier to fire spread, from which to start constructing a fireline. The anchor point is utilized to reduce the chance of being flanked by the fire while the line is being constructed.

AREA COMMAND: An organization established to oversee the management of multiple incidents that are each being handled by an incident management team organization. Area Command has the responsibility to set overall strategy and priorities, allocate critical resources based on priorities, ensure that incidents are properly managed, and that objectives are met and strategies followed.

BACKDRAFT: This is a term applied to the explosion caused by the sudden inward rush of oxygen when all of the super-heated gases in a room or structure, ignite at the same time. If the gasses are pressurized, in a relatively closed room, an explosion could be the result.

BACKFIRE: A fire that is set along the inner edge of a fireline to consume the fuel in the path of a wildfire and/or change the direction or force of the fire's convection column.

BARRIER: Any obstruction to the spread of fire. Usually an area or strip devoid of combustible fuel.

BLOWUP: Sudden increase in fireline intensity or rate of spread of a fire sufficient to preclude direct control or to upset existing suppression plans. Often accompanied by violent convection and may have other characteristics of a firestorm.

BRANCH: The organizational level that has functional or geographical responsibility for major parts of incident operations. The branch level is organizationally between section and division/group in the operations section, and between section and unit in the logistics section.

BRUSH TRUCK / GRAS WAGON etc. – These are vehicles for fighting wildland or grass fires. Some of these are four wheel-drive. Most often this is a tank and a pump mounted on a four wheel drive pick-up.

BURN OUT: Setting fire inside a control line to consume fuel between the edge of the fire and the control line.

BURNING PERIOD: The part of each 24-hour period when fires spread most rapidly; typically from 10:00 A.M. to sundown.

CLOSED AREA: This is an area in which specified activities or entry are temporarily restricted to reduce risk of human-caused fires.

CLOSURE: Legal restriction, but not necessarily elimination, of specified activities such as smoking, camping, or entry that might cause fires in a given area.

COLD TRAILING: This is a method for controlling a partly dead fire edge by carefully inspecting and feeling with the hand for heat to detect any fire, digging out every live spot, and trenching any live edge.

COMMAND STAFF: The command staff consists of the information officer, safety officer and liaison officer. They report directly to the incident commander and may have an assistant or assistants, as needed.

COMPLEX: Two or more individual incidents located in the same general area which are assigned to a single incident commander or unified command.

CONFINE A FIRE: The least aggressive wildfire suppression strategy which can be expected to keep the fire within established boundaries of constructed firelines under prevailing conditions.

CONTAIN A FIRE: A moderately aggressive wildfire suppression strategy which can be expected to keep the fire within established boundaries of constructed firelines under prevailing conditions.

CONTROL LINE: An inclusive term for all constructed or natural barriers and treated fire edges used to control a fire.

COYOTE TACTICS: A progressive line construction duty involving self-sufficient crews which build fireline until the end of the operational period, remain at or near the point while off duty, and begin building fireline again the next operational period where they left off.

CREEPING FIRE: Fire burning with a low flame and spreading slowly.

CROWN FIRE: A fire that advances from top to top of trees or shrubs independent of a surface fire. Crown fires are sometimes classed as running or dependent to distinguish the degree of independence from the surface fire.

CROWN OUT: A fire that rises from ground into the tree crowns and advances from treetop to treetop. To intermittently ignite tree crowns as a surface fire advances.

DIRECT ATTACK: Any treatment applied directly to burning fuel such as wetting, smothering, or chemically quenching the fire or by physically separating the burning from unburned fuel.

DIVISION: Divisions are used to divide an incident into geographical areas of operation. Divisions are established when the number of resources exceeds the span-of-control of the operations chief. A division is located with the ICS organization between the branch and the task force/strike team.

DOZER: Any tracked vehicle with a front mounted blade used for exposing mineral soil.

DOZER LINE: Fireline constructed by the front blade of a bulldozer.

DRAFTING: Pulling water from a source other than a hydrant or another fire apparatus. Cisterns, lakes, ponds and swimming pools are often used in drafting operations. Many departments in rural areas and without fire hydrants use drafting.

ENGINE: Any ground vehicle providing specified levels of pumping, water, and hose capacity but with less than the specified level of personnel.

ESCAPED FIRE: A fire that has exceeded or is expected to exceed initial attack capabilities or prescription.

EXTENDED ATTACK: Situation in which a fire cannot be controlled by initial attack resources within a reasonable period of time. Committing additional resources within 24 hours after commencing suppression action will usually control the fire.

FIRE BEHAVIOR: The manner in which a fire reacts to the influences of fuel, weather, and topography.

FIREBREAK: A natural of constructed barrier used to stop or check fires that may occur, or to provide a control line from which to work.

FIRE EDGE: The boundary of a fire at a given moment.

FIRE EFFECTS: The physical, biological, and ecological impacts of fire on the environment.

FIRELINE: The part of a control line that is scraped or dug to mineral soil. Also called fire trail.

FIRE RETARDANT: Any substance (except plain water) that by chemical or physical actions reduces flammability of fuels or slows their rate of combustion.

FIRE SHELTER: An aluminized tent offering protection by means of reflecting radiant heat and providing a volume of breathable air in a fire entrapment situation.

FLANKS OF A FIRE: The parts of a fire's spread perimeter that are roughly parallel to the main direction of spread.

FLARE-UP: Any sudden acceleration in rate of spread or intensification of the fire. Unlike blowup, a flare-up is of relatively short duration and does not radically change existing control plans.

FLASH FUELS: Fuels such as grass, leaves, draped pine needles, fern, tree moss and some kinds of slash, which ignite readily and are consumed rapidly when dry.

FOAM: The aerated solution created by forcing air into, or entraining air in water containing a foam concentrate by means of suitably designed equipment or by cascading it through the air at a high velocity. Foam reduces combustion by cooling, moistening and excluding oxygen.

FUELBREAK: A natural or manmade change in fuel characteristics which affects fire behavior so that fires burning into them can be more readily controlled.

FUEL TYPE: An identifiable association of fuel elements of distinctive species, form, size, arrangement, or other characteristics that will cause a predictable rate of spread or resistance to control under specified weather conditions.

GENERAL STAFF: The group of incident management personnel reporting to the Incident Commander. They may each have a deputy, as needed. The General Staff consists of: Operation Section Chief, Planning Section Chief, Logistics Section Chief, and a Finance/ Administration Chief.

GROUND FIRE: Fire that consumes the organic material beneath the surface litter ground, such as peat fire.

HAND CREW: A number of individuals that have been organized and trained and are supervised principally for operational assignments on an incident.

HEAD OF A FIRE: The most rapidly spreading portion of a fire's perimeter, usually to the leeward or up slope.

HEAVY FUELS: Fuels of large diameter such as snags, logs, large limb wood, which ignite and are consumed more slowly than flash fuels.

HELD LINE: All control lines that still contain the fire when mop-up is completed. Excludes lost lines, natural barrier not backfired, and unused secondary lines.

HELISPOT: A natural or improved takeoff and landing area intended for temporary or occasional helicopter use.

HOLDOVER FIRE: A fire that remains dormant for a considerable time. Also called sleeper fire.

HOT SPOT: A particularly active part of a fire.

HOTSHOT CREW: Intensively trained fire crew used primarily in hand line construction.

INCIDENT: An occurrence, either human-caused or natural phenomena, that requires action or support by emergency service personnel to prevent or minimize loss of life or damage to property and/or natural resources.

INCIDENT COMMAND POST (ICP): Location at which primary command functions are executed. The ICP may be collocated with the incident base or other incident facilities.

INCIDENT COMMAND SYSTEM: A standardized on-scene emergency management concept specifically designed to allow its user(s) to adopt an integrated organizational structure equal to the complexity and demands of single or multiple incidents, without being hindered by jurisdictional boundaries.

INDIRECT ATTACK: A method of suppression in which the control line is located some considerable distance away from the fire's active edge. Generally done in the case of a fast spreading or high-intensity fire and to utilize natural or constructed firebreaks fuel breaks and favorable breaks in the topography.

INFRARED (IR): A heat detection system used for fire detection, mapping, and hotspot identification.

INITIAL ATTACK: The actions taken by the first resources to arrive at a wildfire to protect lives and property, and prevent further extension of the fire.

KNOCK DOWN: To reduce the flame or heat on the more vigorously burning parts of a fire edge.

LEAD PLANE: Aircraft with pilot used to make trial runs over the target area to check wind, smoke conditions, topography and to lead air tankers to targets and supervise their drops.

MOP-UP: Extinguishing or removing burning material near control lines, felling snags, and trenching logs to prevent rolling after an area has burned, to make a fire safe, or to reduce residual smoke.

OVERHEAD: Personnel assigned to supervisory positions, including Incident Commander, Command Staff, General Staff, Branch Directors, Supervisors, Unit Leaders, Managers, and staff.

PATROL: To travel over a given route to prevent, detect, and suppress fires or to go back and forth vigilantly over a length of control line during and/or after construction to prevent breakovers.

PUBLIC INFORMATION OFFICER (PIO) OR MEDIA INFORMATION OFFICER: In all cases, media information will be handled by command. This is a defined and designated responsibility of the incident commander. This position will be filled or staffed by command. The "Incident Commander" will be the person to give the media information and answer questions or they will detail someone to do this. At times the incident commander will not have time to talk with the media.

REBURN: Repeat burning of an area over which a fire has previously passed, but left fuel that later ignites when burning conditions are more favorable. Also an area that has reburned.

RELATIVE HUMIDITY (RH): The ratio of the amount of moisture in the air, to the maximum amount of moisture that air would contain if it were saturated. The ratio of the actual vapor pressure to the saturated vapor pressure.

RESOURCES: Personnel, equipment, services and supplies available, or potentially available, for assignment to incidents. Personnel and equipment are described by kind and type, e.g., ground, water, air, etc., and may be used in tactical, support or overhead capacities at an incident.

SAFETY ZONE: An area cleared of flammable material used for escape in the event the line is outflanked or in case a spot fire causes fuels outside the control line to render the line unsafe.

SECONDARY LINE: Any fireline constructed at a distance from the fire perimeter concurrently with or after a line already constructed on or near to the perimeter of the fire. Typically constructed as an insurance measure in case the fire escapes control by the primary line.

SIZE UP: A procedure used to assess a situation and report upon it. The first arriving officer on the scene will "give a size-up" over the radio. This will commonly include a description of the structure and the initial plan of attack for combating the fire. Elements may include the time of day, the weather conditions, the availability of water and what may already be known about this structure.

SLASH: Debris resulting from such natural events as wind, fire, or snow breakage; or such human activities as:

- Road construction
- Logging, pruning
- Thinning
- Brush cutting

It includes:

- Logs
- Chunks
- Bark
- Branches

- Stumps
- Broken under-story trees

SMOKEJUMPER: A specifically trained and certified firefighter who travels to wildland fires by aircraft and parachutes to the fire.

SMOLDERING: A fire burning without flame and barely spreading.
SPOT FIRES: Fire ignited outside the perimeter of the main fire by a firebrand.

SPOTTING: Behavior of a fire producing sparks or embers that are carried by the wind and which start new fires beyond the zone of direct ignition by the main fire.

STRIKE TEAM: Specified combinations of the same kind and type of resources, with communications, and a leader.

SUPPRESSION: All the work of extinguishing or confining a fire beginning with its discovery.

SUPPRESSION CREW: Two or more firefighters stationed at a strategic location for initial action on fires. Duties are essentially the same as those of individual firefighters.

SURFACE FIRE: Fire that burns loose debris on the surface, which include dead branches, leaves, and low vegetation.

TACTICS: Deploying and directing resources on an incident to accomplish the objectives designated by strategy.

TASK FORCE: Any combination or single resources assembled for a particular tactical need, with common communications and a leader. A Task Force may be pre-established and sent to an incident, or formed at an incident.

WATER TENDER: Any ground vehicle capable of transporting specified quantities of water.

WILDFIRE: A fire occurring on wildland that is not meeting management objectives and thus requires a suppression response.

WILDLAND: An area in which development is essentially nonexistent, except for roads, railroads, power lines, and similar transportation facilities. Structures, if any, are widely scattered.

CONCLUSION

The competition to become a firefighter can be extremely fierce and it can take significant training to become a firefighter. Even so, this can be a very rewarding career with many benefits. There are also many opportunities for advancement as well as many different categories of firefighting as an industry that can be entered once you have some firefighting experience.

If you are interested in becoming a firefighter, now is the best time to begin preparing for your future career and taking care of the various steps involved in becoming involved in this exciting career opportunity.

To your Success!

Bonus!

Firemen Jokes
(From the book 100% Blonde Jokes by R. Cristi)

A Brunette, a Redhead and a Blonde escape a burning building by climbing to the roof. Firemen are on the street below, holding a blanket for them to jump in.

The firemen yell to the Brunette, "Jump! Jump! It's your only chance to survive!" The Brunette jumps and SWISH! The firemen yank the blanket away. The Brunette slams into the sidewalk like a tomato.

"C'mon! Jump! You gotta jump!" say the firemen to the Redhead.

"Oh no! You're gonna pull the blanket away!" says the Redhead.

"No! It's Brunettes we can't stand! We're OK with Redheads!"

"OK," says the Redhead, and she jumps. SWISH! The firemen yank the blanket away, and the lady is flattened on the pavement like a pancake.

Finally, the Blonde steps to the edge of the roof. Again, the firemen yell, "Jump! You have to jump!"

"No way! You're just gonna pull the blanket away!" yelled the Blonde.

"No! Really! You have to jump! We won't pull the blanket away!"

"Look," the Blonde says. "Nothing you say is gonna convince me that you're not gonna pull the blanket away! So what I want you to do is put the blanket down, and back away from it..."

Other books by Psylon Press:

100% Blonde Jokes
R. Cristi
ISBN 978-0-9866004-1-8

Choosing a Dog Breed Guide
Eric Nolah
ISBN 978-0-9866004-5-6

Best Pictures Of Paris
Christian Radulescu
ISBN 978-0-9866004-8-7

Best Gift Ideas For Women
Taylor Timms
ISBN 978-0-9866004-4-9

Top Bikini Pictures
Taylor Timms
ISBN 978-0-9866426-3-0

Cross Tattoos
Johnny Karp
ISBN 978-0-9866426-4-7

Beautiful Breasts Pictures
Taylor Timms
ISBN 978-1-926917-01-6

For more books please visit:

www.psylonpress.com

CPSIA information can be obtained at www.ICGtesting.com

231605LV00002B/15/P